White for Harvest

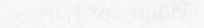

# White for Harvest

## Harvest

### New and Selected Poems

Jeanie Thompson

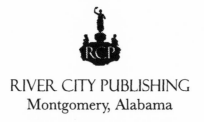

RIVER CITY PUBLISHING
Montgomery, Alabama

Library of Congress Cataloging-in-Publication Data

Thompson, Jeanie.
White for harvest : new and selected poems
/by Jeanie Thompson.
p. cm.
ISBN 0-913515-48-5 (alk. paper)
I. Title.
PS3570.H6254 W47 2001
811'.54—dc21
2001001128

Designed by Lissa Monroe
Printed in the United States of America

*River City publishes books by a variety of distinguished authors and artists. Our imprints include River City, Starrhill, Sycamore, and Black Belt. Our logo is derived from Court Square Fountain in Montgomery, the traditional symbol of our city. The goddess Hebe poses gracefully atop the fountain, facing the nearby Alabama River, and symbolizing prosperity and good fortune for all.*

for Bill

and

in honor of Katherine Wade Thompson
in memory of Byrd Thomas Thompson, Jr.

# Table of Contents

## New poems: *White for Harvest*

December Hawk Flight *North Alabama.* . . . . . . . . . . . . . . . . . 3
Ruth's Song. . . . . . . . . . . . . . . . . . . . . . . . . . . . . . 5
Farewell to a Garden. . . . . . . . . . . . . . . . . . . . . . . . . 6
Earth Hymn . . . . . . . . . . . . . . . . . . . . . . . . . . . . . 8
Gravity, April 1970 . . . . . . . . . . . . . . . . . . . . . . . . . 10
Sluice . . . . . . . . . . . . . . . . . . . . . . . . . . . . . . . 12
In My Father's Workshop . . . . . . . . . . . . . . . . . . . . . . 14
Manhood lights on you . . . . . . . . . . . . . . . . . . . . . . . 15
Two Forms in Echelon *after Barbara Hepworth's sculpture* . . . . 16
Snapshot in the Red Fields . . . . . . . . . . . . . . . . . . . . . 18
The Tightrope Walker's Faith *after Wallenda* . . . . . . . . . . . 19
Elizabeth's Song . . . . . . . . . . . . . . . . . . . . . . . . . . 20
Fragments from Hildegard of Bingen, 1098–1179
    I. First Vision, 1114 . . . . . . . . . . . . . . . . . . . . . 22
    II. Delphinia: The Virgin's Sonnet, 1142. . . . . . . . . . . 23
    III. Letter to Rikkarda, 1162. . . . . . . . . . . . . . . . . 24
At Mt. Nebo Baptist Church *Cusseta, Alabama*. . . . . . . . . . 26

## From *Witness*

Meditation at the Kitchen Window . . . . . . . . . . . . . . . . . 29
Child as Dolphin. . . . . . . . . . . . . . . . . . . . . . . . . . . 30
Young and Old at the Forest Manor Nursing Home . . . . . 31
Lament for Your Face . . . . . . . . . . . . . . . . . . . . . . . . 33
Zodiac. . . . . . . . . . . . . . . . . . . . . . . . . . . . . . . . 34
Weekday Blues for My Son . . . . . . . . . . . . . . . . . . . . . 36

To a Young Brown Belt. . . . . . . . . . . . . . . . . . . . . . . 38
Stars on a Dark Road . . . . . . . . . . . . . . . . . . . . . . 41
The Lyrical Trees . . . . . . . . . . . . . . . . . . . . . . . . 43
Revival . . . . . . . . . . . . . . . . . . . . . . . . . . . . . 44
The Pratt-Mont Drive-In . . . . . . . . . . . . . . . . . . . 46
A Memory of Slaughter . . . . . . . . . . . . . . . . . . . . 48
Slave Gag . . . . . . . . . . . . . . . . . . . . . . . . . . . . 49
Revelation. . . . . . . . . . . . . . . . . . . . . . . . . . . . 50
Ceremony on a Summer Night . . . . . . . . . . . . . . . . 53
A Figure for Truth at Lake Eufaula. . . . . . . . . . . . . . 55

## From *How to Enter the River*

For My Father . . . . . . . . . . . . . . . . . . . . . . . . . . 59
October: The Fact of Trees . . . . . . . . . . . . . . . . . . 61
Obeying My Hands . . . . . . . . . . . . . . . . . . . . . . . 63
At the Wheeler Wildlife Refuge . . . . . . . . . . . . . . . 64
Letters to the Isle of Lesbos . . . . . . . . . . . . . . . . . 66
The Black Venus, 1861 . . . . . . . . . . . . . . . . . . . . 69
Midnight Swim: For Marilyn Monroe . . . . . . . . . . . . 71
His Confession at Mid-afternoon . . . . . . . . . . . . . . . 72
Desire . . . . . . . . . . . . . . . . . . . . . . . . . . . . . . 74
Snowy Egrets Flying Before a Storm . . . . . . . . . . . . 76
After a Winter . . . . . . . . . . . . . . . . . . . . . . . . . 77
Thinking of Kay in Grasmere . . . . . . . . . . . . . . . . . 79
How to Enter the River . . . . . . . . . . . . . . . . . . . . 81

# Acknowledgments

Grateful thanks are given to editors of the following publications in which some of the previously uncollected poems first appeared, some in slightly different forms:

> "December Hawk Flight" and "Elizabeth's Song"
>    —*Alabama Literary Review*
> "Hildegard to Rikkarda" and "Earth Song:
>    Snapshot in the Red Fields"—*Amaryllis*
> "Sluice"—*Black Warrior Review*
> "In My Father's Workshop"—*Southern Humanities
>    Review*
> "Earth Hymn"—*Southern Review*

Several of these poems appeared in *Farewell to a Garden,* a limited edition chapbook printed by Ceil Tanner, China Berry Press, Tuscaloosa, Alabama, 1997.

Other poems herein selected, some slightly revised, are from *How to Enter the River* (Holy Cow! Press, 1985) and *Witness* (Black Belt Press, 1995).

New poems: *White for Harvest*

# December Hawk Flight
*North Alabama*


In this moment
hard with rapture
the pair of hawks
wheels from the winter tree,
parting above us, crying
to one another
as they circle,
their reconnaissance of power
dwarfing the northern field
where a mouse
throbs in the stubble—
its fear freezing
to a brush stroke.

From treetop to treetop
across the fields
they signal one another—

You want to taste
that tongue of air
lifting her as she
wheels free of him.
I want to descend as he falls
to earth, rising again

with him, the heartblood
cooling in his talons.

I want the clarity
of her wingpull
as she inverts air,
willing it to take her
into the red wash
of feather and prey.
You want to glide
in his shadow,
covered, and covering
his strength
in your plummet.

They wheel
from the bare tree
above us,
signaling danger.
We turn toward
one another—
alive in their clarity,
their blood,
our ascending hearts.

# Ruth's Song

As One who looked upon
the face of the deep found
mystery, and drew a circle,
we circle the field,
find before us a mystery
plucked from nothingness.

We breathe it to life,
as tangible as roasted grain.
I know you, my husband,
as the reaper winnows,
tossing the sheaf heavenward
so that the summer air
bears away chaff
the human heart dares not collect.

Here on the threshing floor,
we lift the grain to heaven,
believing the wind, that sustaining
breath, will bear our lives—
and scatter them—
so that we fall gently to the harvest
of each other's arms.

# Farewell to a Garden

All I crave is a leaf's sheen
after sudden rain,
the tenderest frond
of spiderwort just beyond
the mossy border.
And when summer light
fails all around me
and I cup
the shoot of crepe myrtle,
I know if I am
anything at all,
it is fern, forsythia,
a woman who dreams
the fiddlehead's
unfurling,
blesses the twin flags
of the seed's release.

And when the world darkens
and fireflies announce
earth's bountiful tipping
toward indifferent night,
I can believe
nothing is left behind
where water and earth

mediate in a language
too fine for humans,
unless they seek
the true tamping down
of a gardener's charmed footfall
that says *promise,*
*life continuing,*
*what belongs returns.*

# Earth Hymn

The tines caked with mud amaze
       him he says and then as the April afternoon
wanes he turns the earth and pours in humus
       *I cannot open the earth and not think of you*
in the backyard near the old oak
       set like an elephant's giant foot in my
tree-ring garden I'm on my knees
       deep in the one act I know brings
peace he is up front with the child who delights
       in nightcrawlers a bucketful of fish bait though we have
no water nearby the days I came upon
       your entourage furiously at work in your garden
they rallied around your heart
       toting impossible weights of rock and dirt
your sweet father covered in mud
       on his knees saying "Is this where Stephanie wanted
the begonias?" you would appear then
       sun hat over the wig to take me on a tour
"here is the rare Japanese maple we found—
       next year these will come back fuller"
in the evening he will go out one last time
       to the back garden some errand
that can't wait until first light and return to
       hold me and say "I feel the garden humming"
I push the earth down and think I should tamp

it the way you did walking methodically
down the rows to pack tighter that rich dirt
        from which later in the year the hollyhock towered
the moonbeam coreopsis floated in its ferns
        and you began the transformation
each morning breathing the day
        opening the earth I will think of you

# Gravity, April 1970

The aerodynamic miracle
of the bumblebee as he plunders
blue-stalked salvia this summer morning
holds me like gravity, as the pollen's lure

holds him. But wings lift and he tumbles
forth, appears to wander
among the other blossoms, returning
to dock at the hive, deliver his store.

When the dazed astronaut, Lovell, freed from his orbit
and cast asunder
by a ruined coil and twist of fate, squinted
into the Pacific light, I was still not sure

that I could break the circle,
loose the bonds of home and wander
alone, among my disparate selves, losing
everything in freedom's release—weightless, pure.

The oracle
I swore I deciphered under
the din of pain, and the shimmering,
centrifugal lure

of youth spoke a simple miracle:
home beckons us to break free, as the blossom's plunder
lures the bee, of a summer morning,
to its blue and fragile shore.

# Sluice

Your boy is a river
whose current takes you ever
nearer, ever far
from the palpable shore
of your heart.
This summer he sleeps long
hours, his golden hair streaked
with sweat and sun
in waning days of imagined
innings, slide and catch,
brave hours while he waits
for you to watch him
enact the fantastic
cannonball, his legs
surging in the private
waters of dream.
Now naturalist
with a bug among
the scuppernongs,
now hero, conquistador
of backyard and sunset.
How will you open the perfecting
locks of your wish for him
so he can tumble his sure waters,
sluice the gate as free

as the moment you made him?
Hold him as lightly
as good beads cling to his brow,
those drops tasting of salt,
of your river,
the day's golden summer, now.

# In My Father's Workshop

Here is the last box he made: cherry wood,
aged to a warm auburn, silken as a girl's hair.

Dovetails, not quite flush, graze
my fingers as I smooth the wood

he brushed with turpentine,
easing it into the grain's part

with long strokes of steel wool.
Lifting the lid, I measure

the blade's marks that ripple
like fine waves.

Inside floats a nest of papery
shavings, young cherry wood

planed to curls.
I scoop these up to my face, bending

to breathe their life.
Her delighted laughter rises

from the open box
like a brown-throated wren.

# Manhood lights on you

like a gift, and it's as if someone jerks
my head back and says, "Look again, he changed,
is changing, and you can see it—now
*look! Quick!*"

And there you are standing on the porch
in the newly washed shirt of yourself, your
boy-Man self, like a shirt rinsed and pinned up
to dry: there the sharp angle of cheekbone,
horizon of straight shoulders, here the flat chest
and tickle of hair on your lip. It shines on you
like a mailed suit. I glimpse it—can almost
knock the metal of it—then

it's gone and you slouch like a slit sack
of flour, spilling onto the couch
in an attitude of disdain for the world,
me, anything the enemy camp might dish out.

Now I hold the sharp frame of a young man,
ready to have the world hang from you
like a general's sash, bravery flowing like light—
Shall I tell you, touch you, or just shield my eyes?

# Two Forms in Echelon
*after Barbara Hepworth's sculpture*


Walking once in Cornwall
in the garden Hepworth cast—
bronze forms undulating like Yorkshire hills
by England's rugged Southern coast—
I found them: *two forms in echelon.*
Solid selves, yet she had scooped each
open to a chalk-white core
where light and air circled
like a dancer's arms,
containing space, and releasing it.

Later, I wandered in another garden
and came upon them again.
Their bronze forms green and upright
and noble in the early spring light.
As clearly as the water rippling
in the garden's blue mosaic pool,
I recognized

that their bond—this tender echelon—
was the inclination of their strength,
the rounder one slightly curving
toward its thinner, stalwart mate.
As I walked around them,

the clarifying light poured
through their open forms,
and I saw that they were shaped
by spirit palpable as bronze,
and witnessed their union—
literal as air.

# Snapshot in the Red Fields

The dirt cakes his boot soles as he steps down from the machine
        idling now in the field the sun slants toward evening and the smell
of damp, just-turned earth fills him so that he thinks he will burst with it
        ˙he must stop and look, now, before the daylight leaves the county,
before the hawk spreads its wings one last time, drops into a row
        and disappears over the grove of trees the machine coughs once, a dirty
cloud of diesel plumes into the air he sifts the earth through his fingers,
        something he can't touch often enough impossible to explain to her,
to anyone, how the fields keep him alive, and at these moments, when
        the plow has turned the rows and the earth is open before him in its deep
moist iron-rich splendor, he would just as soon dive into it and forget
        himself, down, down into its depth, rather than ever lose it or know
that the season would not come again

# The Tightrope Walker's Faith
*after Wallenda*

If one man on the street below
holding this cable
shifts on the ball of his foot,
I will feel the wire give like envy.
As I slide one rosined foot past
the other, the tempest
of buildings calms around me.
Like Peter, I step out
into my horizonless sea,
hearing everything—
the rush of water through a pipe,
the rooftop flutter
of a pigeon,
the click of a small heart
not stopping out of fear.
This is all to Your glory—
but steady—
one pulse following the other.

# Elizabeth's Song

It was in the morning, just over
the swell of hills spread out before me,
you came walking, a small, steady figure

brightening the landscape. *See!*
you cried, your breath
coming steady, *Do you see?*

In that moment, belief
was a small foot knocking hard
at my ribs, the earth's

slow circle, the wide world
sharpening, a voice
welling from the child

inside me: *I am with you,*
*wonder no more.* I took your hand.
Grace lit you

and the fire no man
has felt leapt
through us. Men wrote later

that the babe leapt
in me for joy, but it was
power, mercy

at the source, the error
forever made straight,
steady as one pulse tuning

itself to another:
*heart of God  heart of man*
*heart of God  heart of man*

# Fragments from Hildegard of Bingen, 1098–1179

## I. First Vision, 1114

I saw our Lord as water
tumbling down the face
of the cliff rock.
He spoke to me clearly,
saying, *Take Jutta's hand.*
*Your mother now,*
*she will lead you to me.*
He parted the waterfall
so that I glimpsed
the window circling his face,
chips of ruby, sapphire, emerald.
His eyes spoke to me
of sorrow, but such joy!
He said *Come,*
*Hildegard, this world is yours—*
*your hands to serve,*
*your eyes, these windows.*

## II. Delphinia: The Virgin's Sonnet, 1142

Here is young Delphinia at our gate,
her stomach so large with child

she bears no resemblance to the girl
I witnessed kneeling

just last winter in Vespers. The gray wool
of her dress stretches across the dull belly—

life engendered in her by a brutish
husband. Anger fills me like an unwanted offering.

I turn its coins toward heaven, the Virgin's light
never so necessary, never so true

as today when I walk among what these women I lead
have made and consider the egg inside me,

how it pronounces its one syllable
of love for Him, through Her.

## III.  Letter to Rikkarda, 1162

This morning I harvested plums
so heavy their stems yielded to the weight.
You would have smiled to see this,
keeping your silence.

At Vespers I lead the women
toward purer articulation of His love,
but I am caught by the sweet odor
of four o'clocks, these distractions
sown as renegades and watered in secret
by a novice longing for her mother's garden.

Rikkarda, at this hour when I see
my soul's release, I am pulled
toward memory: your sure-footed
tamping of fresh earth before plants
were set in spring. You parsed
weeds from useful herbs, your purpose
sure as you tended young rosemary,
the fragrant tarragon you loved,
and penny royal to lay across my brow
when pain blinded me.

As the sun dips behind our mountains tonight,
I kneel to confess: I cannot count you gone,
yet cannot feel your here, and in this agony

of doubt when color drops
from the bee balm's urgent flame—
its first fire so like your spirit—
I know it is toward you, Rikkarda, I turn.

# At Mt. Nebo Baptist Church
*Cusseta, Alabama*

Across the not-quite-fall pastures the hawks call and fly to one another
      rustling the meadowlark alerting the mockingbird both brought
to song's light by the greater bird's coarse cry a box turtle lumbers
      across the county pavement and disappears into a clutch
of yellow pieweed against the fence a last long look across the pasture
      and deep in-breath of morning light before we enter
the neat brick church amid greetings warm hands shaking ours
      *Ask someone to start the congregational song* an elder commands
above the not-quite-fall pastures the voice rises guttural and keening
      to the five black men in straight chairs facing the worshippers
throwing the song up and catching it tossing the harvested bolls
      into the sack of memory tossing the song to us I close my eyes
the tenor to my left takes me along his row I look up hear the hawk cry
      feel the bloodsongs smell the scuffed red dirt pull the fiber of song
expertly free the knowledge I witness the keening uttered
      and answered here in 1998 in Mt. Nebo Church in Cusseta, Alabama
my ears his mouth we are loved we are forgiven we are loved we are everyone forgiven

from *Witness*

# Meditation at the Kitchen Window

To look up and out is the point. Today, the rain
      we need has fallen, finally, slow and steady.
Two hundred miles away a hurricane drags
        the coast, and whole lives are whisked away
            like a scattering of toys.
Here at the window, I'm almost aware
      of my part in all this.
            I can watch the roses' progress—yesterday
in tight buds, today flaring
      salmon in the wind. Lately, a strand
        of winter weed has ascended
the canes, and again and again
      I have sent myself out to strip it back,
        seek the root and pull it whole from the ground.
And I could stand here, in the repetition
      of what I must witness
        and what I hope to change
if it were not for your cry
      which causes me to turn, my son, from the window.

# Child as Dolphin

In the almost empty tub tonight
you stretched out
full-length on your stomach,
your back to me,
your arms straight above your head,
suddenly deep in a ritual all your own.
And then I pulled you
backwards by your feet
over the smooth porcelain
and your laughter rippled the air.
I cannot know how you knew
to do this, but like the dolphin
who follows a ship for the pleasure
of moving in its wake,
you pressed your small body
against the slick tub again and again,
and I took your ankles
in my hand and pulled you backwards
over and over to hear
the laughter—as if I could
hold the clear sound that flowed
through the fingers of my hand.

# Young and Old at the Forest Manor Nursing Home

I spoon peas into your mouth
and he eats ice cream brought for another,
flings himself full length

on the hospital bed and grins at us while you say,
"Let him be . . . just let him be."
Your hand sweeps out encompassing

the roses blooming before you,
"I never knew them to be so beautiful."

I help you pick your way
through a landscape of memory
tangled with present clutter.

A sentence is not an easy step—
A freak wind through trees, a bloom wildly
out of time, a cloud shaping itself

into something to recognize, then lose.
And to him can you be more than this?
A doll of sticks strapped in your chair.

Ah, but he is full of the present
and will kiss you as many times
as I repeat,

"Tell Mrs. Wright you love her,"
and you pull him
to the bone and breath of you again.

# Lament for Your Face

After the story
when you have cast off into sleep,
I lie close to your face, watching
as the man you will become
enters you,

and I imagine how this beauty
will cause someone pain.
Thinking how
the legs and arms will lengthen,
the skin toughen, the beard grow,
until, when your eyes open again,
there will be another woman
gazing at you closely
and she will smile

and you will smile as you reach for her,
not caring when
you last slept.

# Zodiac

Nothing in my story will satisfy
the engine of your longing
to know her, little boy filled
with the fiercest wonder.

Tonight, on our way home,
I made my way again
by explanation's crude map. This time:
telling the twelve houses of the zodiac,

naming the signs of all your kin, friends.
*He's Cancer, she's Leo, I'm Aquarius.*
Then your question stopped me
like an unexpected turn:

What is my real mother's sign?
The car filled with her shadowy
presence as you grappled
to uncover the road back to her.

Myth-maker still, I said a story:
when you were born
your mother cut the cord from you,
and from her slippery world,

buried it—then gave me
the clue. I whispered to the man
who lay beside me,
now, it is time to find our son.

But you were already in motion,
approaching us
as the constellation of your life
spiraled overhead, and we knew.

We turned to thank
the exacting, curious stars
crossing and uncrossing
to reveal the path.

# Weekday Blues for My Son

Sitting in the unexpectedly pleasant
afternoon light of Taco Casa,
I watched your eyes
deepen to a blue
reserved for a lover's dive,
not a mother's eyes
at 6:27 p.m.
with Boy Scouts three minutes away.
I was irrational with fatigue,
and that question surfaced again,
Where is the man with these eyes
who held her long enough
to conceive you, then was gone?

When these emotions collided in me
like commuters piling up on 15th Street
there was a flush of tears I pushed back—
so unwelcome here, at this moment
of your blue eyes. I didn't want to cry.
I wanted to be as beautiful as you!
But I knew what you saw in that flash-photo
children shoot and hold in their hearts:
a woman who looked strained

and somehow sad as she ate a taco,
though you didn't linger here.

Perhaps it was the sweetness
of that collision
that made me want to hold it,
sneak one more look into your eyes
while the afternoon sun filled them
with color rare as peace.
Perhaps I wanted to feel that pain
so that losing you will be familiar,
and, therefore, possible to endure.

# To a Young Brown Belt

A child, surely
you are only a child,
you move with the grace
of a flower opening,
arms and legs quick
as lightning strikes.
The inspiration of each
breath like water
poured over steaming coals.

Your mother and I
sit on the steps,
two friends
watching her son,
as you dance your way
through the shu-sen kata.
Neighborhood flowers
applaud for backdrop
like incongruous elders.

Such power
in such a small body
is more amazing
than one hundred sen-seis.
But you are not amazed.
You have practiced
until pain is play, knuckles

one with the driveway
where you offer
push-ups in July heat.

Your brown cap of hair
dampened to the scalp, cheeks
flushed as they might be
later from love,
you jump and kick,
twirling in the air
like a small dervish
above the manicured lawn.

Just this month,
your mother has told you
her secret
and you understand
the next level.
So you will face this enemy
with which you have been paired—
your breath withheld
till the last second possible, when,
releasing the energy
to the center
of Its
being,

you believe you can defeat Death,
and bow
to the one who gave you life.


*for Stephen Skipper, and in memory of Stephanie Skipper*

# Stars on a Dark Road

Here we are again—I'm at the wheel
on a clear night, on a dark road.
I lean over, look up
and see the stars, the bright stars
that are always there.
I'm dreaming with my eyes open
of the bluffs above the Sipsey River,
the hush of silt in low water
brushing the canoe bottom,
the proud stands of royal fern
on the outcroppings of rock,
and the delicate flower of alligator grass,
undisturbed.

You taught me to be still for these.
Tonight moving through darkness,
I think of you.

In class I might've tangled for an hour
with the simple metaphor of a poem
but for one long cold day you called out "right, left"
and "left, left" from the back of the boat.
Survival. And true reciprocity.

Catalpa, wild magnolia, its leaves wide as sleeves,
bouquets of purple phlox and sunny coreopsis.
You would appreciate these,
though your laughter might belie it.

I'm led forward by stars on a dark road,
though sleep threatens to take me
in its current. I have no idea
really, where I am. The stars, like your voice
in the boat behind me. Oldest guides,
bearers of the world's patience.

*for Becky Contois*

# The Lyrical Trees

It's winter and we've turned once again
to the landscape for some scrap of truth
to confound us, to show us who we are.
But the land is cold, burrowed deep into itself this winter.
A brown furze covers the pastures where cattle
huddle against one another in the bitter, afternoon light.
Across the ground, around the deserted house,
over the trees, the vines of summer make a ghost network
holding fast for spring. It's all set
to pull us down, into its slow metabolism, all but these three,
rising in twists that dancers dream to imitate,
in love with this season
when their beautiful bare limbs, their smooth bark
can sing and move upward in the shattering air.

# Revival

The seats were rough to the touch,
plain board planks where a finger
could pick up a mean splinter.
Under our feet, sawdust kicked up
our noses, and dust filtered
in the light from bare bulbs
swinging in the autumn heat.
I listened to a man spout words
that threatened to choke,
to devour me with love. He was
in pain, wracked with the love
he spoke about as I worked
at the splinter in my thumb.
He begged me to come forward
and I wanted to go
but my feet ground the sawdust
and I sat in my seat like a rock.
There must've been a boy I spied
who was cute enough to distract
me from the weeping man, but I
don't remember any boy. What
stays with me after thirty years
of remembering is raw fear.
Fear of sitting on the rough plank
all night, of the crying man

whose florid face and weeping eyes
saw only me. And of how I cried
in my bed that night as my mother
tutored a neighbor boy in Spanish
—*uno, dos, tres*—
not knowing I too
was breaking my way through
a language of fire, and life
everlasting that looked so good
I didn't dare move.

# The Pratt-Mont Drive-In

1.
You must enter the tattered drive
past a fountain of lights,
stilled now at midday.
Take in your hand the rusted chain
and heft of padlock, then step over.

You were always here at twilight,
twirling with your brother
on the tilted, spinning playground disk.
Skinny arms holding on, your head hung back
and you saw the world upside down,
dragged a foot where foul water pools now.
Back in the Ford, you peered over the seat,
then dozed, dreaming a succession
of taillights and the screen returned to silence.


2.
You seek the detail
in corners, the shafts of light,
the exact angle of the exit signs
that repeat after each row.
And the big screen, its placards separating

against a backdrop of humid, milky sky,
blank, offers nothing.

Ask yourself the question,
add the details again and again.
See yourself driving in at eight o'clock,
autumn, the car warm, the boy
ready for anything. Smell the first
cigarette, the beery taste of his lips,
the soft focus of men and women larger than life.
And you, holding your breath, wondering,
*how* long *did that kiss last?*

# A Memory of Slaughter

Down the hill she would come, bearing the struggling,
white-feathered thing. At the Chinaberry stump, grandfather
lifted the ax. I stood back, listening
for the fretful, dumb noises it made.

Now I try to get the stain just right,
blood streaking the sidewalk, the apple tree, Trixie's doghouse.
It was here Allen threw the dagger like a pirate,
pinning my foot to the ground. The cool hands
of Grandmother pull it clean, tighten then loosen
the tourniquet to save my life.

I look through the hickory smoke to see my brothers
holding the cane poles for high jump, taunting
and laughing at each other. Grandmother wrestles
the chicken to the stump. Grandfather lifts his ax.
I turn away, sick with the smell of blood,

and hear my brother scream, his arm snaps, the chicken's
neck cracks, and feathers cloud the November air.
The landscape blurs like charcoal.
She gathers me into her bloodstained arms.

# Slave Gag

Heavy, heavy in my hand, like an iron horseshoe
hammered flat, with a small tongue inside it
to rest on the tongue of a person
who should be quiet, gagged.
In fifth grade we didn't understand the abstraction, *slave*,
but I knew that this horror I was holding
had been intended for someone
with a mouth for talking, for singing,
for saying something when it was time to be quiet.

There in the classroom
I tried to imagine it in a mouth,
in a person working in a field, in my mouth,
on my tongue, but my mind
spit out the image because it could
weigh the heft of that thing in my hand,
or touch what once touched someone
who stood in a field wanting desperately to sing
or curse the empty sky.

# Revelation

You come back as if the deep green
cover of leaf upon leaf could show you.

Once the land was parted, cleared
and dug for those who came before.
Trees fell and rose again as beams
or took shape in thresholds.
Fire rippled across grass,
barbed wire ran like vine for miles.
And the gentle hands, the strong
gentle hands, tended all.

You step onto the porch, reaching for
the rusted screen to learn whose breath
filled the rooms, who sang on the porch
as mist filled the pastures at dusk,
who whispered his lies
underneath a tattoo of summer rain.
Standing where someone once looked
from his doorway to see his life disappearing,
you are certain there is a cry
distinct as the taste of thunder
at the back of your throat.

What draws you to this landscape
is more than shelter, past usefulness.
You would turn the lens

of your desire toward the scene
but always the sun is harsh, the shadows hardest
at 6 o'clock. The questions ripen
like early summer fruit. Whose hands
wrapped themselves inside an apron
when there was no one to call back to?
What child spooned red dirt under this porch
and watched a horse, or the image of a horse,
disappearing into the blue light of summer?
And what joy welled up easy to run pure
over the creekbed of hope?

Listening to the redwing's cry,
skimming the hayfield at twilight,
you know it won't come, no matter how long
you stand breathing the odor of decay.
What has drawn you here opens out
beyond this porch, this planet,
to let you see yourself,
like the one whose presence seizes you.

It is as simple as the promise you make
as you strip a length of vine from the window frame,
and later when you turn to step down from the porch.
You had come to find a sign of someone you might

recognize among what was abandoned.
In the dust-washed light of the window panes
the eyes you see are yours.

# Ceremony on a Summer Night

It is not the particular flower
that helps me remember you—
but the way you tended that plant, watering
it from your aluminum pitcher each evening
in the relentless heat of August, September
and into October—the month of your birth.

From your porch you could watch the neighborhood
coalesce at dusk. The boy toddling
to your door to demand a cookie
now moves past your house.
I hold both our memories.
You should not be gone.

Tonight—in the story time hour—racing
gently to separate grass from flowers in the wet earth,
I sifted the dirt of my garden
over and over in my fingers, marking the place
where I would plant your flower—
that lilac-colored one you loved.

Then I went to your garden wall, dug four stalks,
and walked home a thief.
I cupped a handful of your garden's dirt

for luck. Sprinkling it in, I said a prayer,
"May I be remembered in such a way."

Just then
the fireflies opened their lamps
in cadence to nothing in particular,
save hearts that care for flowers,
neighbors, all.


*For Stella Wright, 1896–1992*

# A Figure for Truth at Lake Eufaula

Caught in the spell of winter's colors,
we talked, tempting twin ghosts
*sadness* and *regret* from low-hanging

mist across backwater
that mirrored skeletal trees
where we walked. Remembering

loving someone
years ago, I saw that your hand
could be

like his hand, your
strength like his strength.
How, when we thought we could

least desire, desire reappeared.
Waterbirds flew at our approach.
Here, you admitted you understood

the hunter's drive to strike, and I
gave evidence that I knew how
the hunted fly, how the wings pump,

the body lightens toward the updraft.
Then I knew, but couldn't say: the past
is not about loss. Not merely loss,

but was like a field we walked out of,
cracking the stock to spill the unspent shells,
quieting to watch the feathers splay open

as beauty, bent on survival. Knowing
forgiveness of ourselves
as a figure for truth.

from *How to Enter the River*

# For My Father

The child you hold
sits wide awake,
rapt, for *Scuppers the Sailor Dog.*
For you the words form
regularly into patterns
bound between the covers
of this Little Golden Book.
But for her, there are no words,
though sounds paint the sailor dog
asleep in his cabin, on his ship,
sailing his own sea.

I want to sit on the bed's edge
and listen.
You see, but motion me away.
Still, I raise the spyglass
and the world's soft features
align themselves.

I wish we could reach back
across the water,
the pine-green sea of the story,
and touch
like two heads bowed above a book.
I wish I could pull on the garment

of Scuppers's character
as she wore it, for warmth,
for imagined safety,
as she entered his world
and her own, forming one word,
crossing the water into sleep.

# October: The Fact of Trees

### I.

In Alabama, memory peels the yellowed
photograph of your father.
He is still young, handsome in his bowler hat.
All his brothers are smiling as if
he's the one who'd told the joke. The fact of him
will not change, though we leave the cemetery
where one red tree flames out of itself.

You want to drive further north,
to see the red and gold and purple,
those leaves that blush now
a new, unfamiliar color.
The wind will carry them off
and you find yourself chasing them.

You might dig the clay for the colors
but the grit, worked under your fingernails,
comes alive in your skin at night.
In dreams you tear at gloves of pain
grown like bark to your hands,
impossible as memory to be stripped clean.

### II.

This year a foreign autumn kisses
and steals the trees. It is Indian summer.
The birches that border the yard flame gold,

then drop their leaves overnight.
You would throw them back to the trees
but the colors burn your fingers.

Firs and pines hold armfuls of snow
as an offering. Even these do not satisfy,
Standing green and blue all winter. You know
their needles are sharp, sticky with resin,
though they hold this heavy blanket of snow up to you:
A gesture like wind layering snow
in New England, rain in Alabama.

I see faces in the leaves
the way children see things at night.
I know the leaves are leaves,
as the child does, but see the faces still.
When I think of you
it is at that point
between the leaf and the face,
between memory
and the fact that you are not here.

*For my mother*

# Obeying My Hands

What lets me forget you?
Nothing.
Tonight as I scrub the copper pot,
I know you'll never do this again.
How simple a thing to remember you by—
but you are in me as I circle
the sponge efficiently in soap,
will the pot to come clean.
These could be your hands.
*Move, work, move,* they tell me,
and I do it,
because I can make no sense
of your dying, or my hands,
little masters, urging me on.


*In memory of Kay Dorsch*

# At the Wheeler Wildlife Refuge

## I. The Observation Building

The little girl in line for the telescope
says, "Look! Them birds are black pepper!"
and turns, grinning, surprised at herself.
Beyond the wall of glass, the flock
rises to light across the bare river bank.

"That bird's crazy," someone whispers.
But the sparrow hawk is dancing in place
fifty yards up, wings beating
as if its power draws nothing from the earth.
For a second its wings flash
open, stilled, then it dances again
and falls from sight.

## II. Walking the Trail

Winter wheat, rabbit tobacco, sorghum
dried to a dark rattle.
Harvest of sparse color in a dry wind.
And thorns low on the ground,
a network of warning.
Beyond this miniature trail, cornfields

64

spread green in winter grass.
I stop walking to face the far-off, solid
stand of pines. I tilt my head back:
the air is sweet. Closing my eyes,
I breathe again,
there's no other word,
so I lay my head back, breathing
as deep as a blue-tick hound
when the scent floods past
rank and scared for life.
When I leave this place
I'll take the four-lane
cutting through the backwater.
What tells me I'm alive
is impossible, useless to carry away.

# Letters to the Isle of Lesbos

I.
This shell of the hawksbill won't warm into song
for you or anyone, these strings

and our separation make things clearer,
clouding the past like the tortoise-shell's

milky reds, yellows, and browns.
Today I've walked for hours through cypresses

tossed by a late summer wind.
I long for the stillness of olive groves

heavy with fruit, a song for you,
I would sing just for you,

my fingers barely touching the strings.

Once I saw a girl gathering jonquils and anemone.
She chose blossoms for her hair

bright as torchlight.
It was then I closed my eyes

and the wind became a voice
carrying my song,

pressing against her,
molding the soft shapes of her tunic.

I imagined her translucent skin
growing warm at this touch.

When the sun fell,
like a coin dropped for luck into the Aegean,

I could believe in signs from heaven
as pure as the song rising from the warm sea

touching a young girl who knows nothing.

II.
I dreamed your mouth was the lotus flower
opening in a kiss.
Your lips were pale petals tinged with silver.
As I brush my hair loose,
the feel of it lifting off my shoulders
with the night wind
is like your hand, reaching to pull me back.
Tonight no one notices me walking alone
along the shore.
Rocks bruise my bare feet.
Night opens on the marble cliffs,
specters flicker, indistinct as the dead,
gone when the creamy moon rises . . .

We lay on the bleached rock
and couldn't speak. My nightdress

67

dampening on the beach.
You loosened the purple band
from my loop of hair.
Against your warm skin
the moon was a light breath.
I believed for that moment
she was benevolent,
covering us with soft, yellow light.

But tonight, beside the black pool
of the sea, the moon seeps into my skin.
In a country as far away as death,
you walk toward me. Your arms, strong
as the limbs of an olive tree, lift me
to be kissed, but the moon's fragrant lips
touch my eyes in sleep.
As you lower me to the rocks
I take no notice
if they welcome me with small gifts,
jewels of purple and black. I am joining you

along Acheron, to watch the moist flower open.

# The Black Venus, 1861

If I dress for you in cheap, stage jewels
unwinding this coarse, black hair to my breasts,
I forget that the theatre was half-full tonight
of drunks and garish women,
the young men who always smell of wine or urine
standing outside the door,
throwing paper flowers at my feet.

You place a giant bowl of milk
at my feet and ask me to drink from it
like a cat with my pink tongue. You say
my hands are rough and beg me
to stroke your poor, tired head.
The lines you read while unbuttoning

your shirt mean nothing.
It is enough for the wine and what
I like better. Later, if you stay
I may allow you to curl on my breasts
tangling my hair for comfort, muttering curses
because you think you are near my heart.

If I close my eyes
there is a deep black forest

where a lover brings me fruit.
The sound of wind
through the broad-leaved trees is cool
and the perfume in my blood tells me
who I am and what I have always been.

# Midnight Swim: For Marilyn Monroe

Night for you is the deep violet
rising from Victorian brownstones
in twilight Manhattan.
But here in Hollywood, each dive is pure gold
and the water shedding your skin, alive.
Where once every barroom wall
held a blonde nude on crimson velvet,
now you step from flesh-colored tights
to toss silver dollars at the screen.

Unable to sleep you float
in a pink diaphanous nightgown
through studio streets, returning
to the camera, still trusting
only its clear eye reversing you.
And facing the best of friends,
a hundred feet of silent color film,
you wink and dive
rising with a laugh.
Your platinum star spills into darkness
and is lost returning.

71

# His Confession at Mid-afternoon

All day I dug the creek bed for your colors.
I wanted to cover your face with a mask
of raw sienna. I wanted to cast
your laughter in rose madder.
But color couldn't hold the light of a star
as its spark took life in you

running up to me through the creek.
I offer white canvas to dry your legs
as you spread the wet skirt on the grass.
How long since
you sat simply for me by the window,
removed your purple felt hat, letting
your hair fall over one eye.
Where it touched your shoulder
I called it Indian yellow.

You were warm and slipped the satin scarf
from your long muscular throat.
My fingers later left a flush
I couldn't paint. I wanted only
the colorless wash of air and skin.
This morning
I took the camel-hair brushes

and rinsed each one in the creek,
stirring for a trace of blond or indigo

but your face would not appear.
Now as I lie here, still, inside you,
I don't need to say your hair
feels like thick wheat against my cheek,
or your skin smells like rain.

# Desire

The dream repeats its motif:
I reach toward you but you move
through my gesture
even as you turn your face away.
A young woman skirts the edge;
she only complicates
what we cannot change.

What does it mean to have lost you,
one I never had?

Last time we were together
I sat talking with you,
managing the conversation
like a tangible burden we share.
Once in a silence, I wanted to smooth
my hands over your whole body
to make sure you were there, become
what I knew you to be.

I watched desire, as if it can exist apart,
like a squall approaching over water.
At the edge of the thunderclouds
I saw rain, imagined
mist dampening my arms

as the wind picked up.
Suddenly I was on the other side.
I turned and saw behind me
the blue-gray filaments moving away
as the storm delivered to the land
its sheer, ardent body.

# Snowy Egrets Flying Before a Storm

Thunderclouds gathered above the highway
like a bruise rising to the surface of the sky.
I crossed the Mississippi and rain fell,
the world became water, gray matter.

In the stillness just ahead of the storm
I saw snowy egrets lifting above a field.
Their bodies rose, a chorus
catching the currents of the mightier air.
Their flock twisted and whipped,
a delicate net of feather, wing and bone
that broke as the storm flew into them
and I felt the fear hold me
and I flew with it.

# After a Winter

We drove through the Blue Ridge,
our first visit after a long separation,
your body healing at last.
Broom sedge shifted like winter wheat
among the gray trees.
We climbed higher, and saw below us
the mountains like a herd of camels
who'd strayed into Virginia.
Kneeling, their long necks tucked down,
they slept in the foreign earth.
How did I know you were forgiving
a child lost to you?

Later, in the bare maples
four young does
grazed close to the highway.
When I asked, you stopped the car.
Each dipped her head in turn
and blinked fathomless eyes.
I rolled down the window
to make a noise in my throat,
as close as I could come to praying.
Catching the human scent
one stepped nearer,
raised a delicate neck,

signaled her white tail
as if a calf were there.
The cold suspended us
and I heard every stillness
in her body cry *live*.

*for A. M. G.*

# Thinking of Kay in Grasmere

On an afternoon like this
      you taught me afternoon tea
            but I never knew why you poured milk
over the back of a spoon into your cup.
      Something British, a habit I witnessed,
          but never understood.

Kay, it's spring here, green everywhere.
      The fig tree abloom in her gauzy leaves
            as if life were all green infusion.
I am afraid of not saying what I mean:
      you are dying;
         I won't see you again.

After school, I boil water, warm the pot,
      exhausted, thinking how today I saw words
            skip and dodge just out of my grasp.
Children's faces, skin taut and clear.
      Tentative, one handed me a poem,
          pressed his small body against mine.

Remember our talks about children?
      The children I'll never know,
         your daughter's you'll never see.
Who are these people? Thoughts we conjure?

I want to ask hard if they're real,
             or have any meaning, because today I know

you near that place where all
             unborn children are. I could
                    imagine mine, blond and fair,
or dark in their secret habits, but what
             use is that? I've done with them, living apart,
                    lost in their own world.

Last night I dreamed of England,
             the country where I'd hope to see you
                    delighting in the bright cardinals you love.
Today, my hands gesture as if to touch your face—
             I would pour strong tea in a china cup,
                    I would define the exact angle of yellow-

skirted daffodils in sunlight. Pitilessly, the world
             shines on into spring, in New Orleans, where
                    one living child dreams the image for *sunrise*.
He picks his words eagerly, breathing them
             in and out, the simple choice
                    all that is necessary, friend, for speech.

# How to Enter the River

Now the singing of the river is his.
He has opened his eyes and each tree
in its green integrity
bows as he moves past.
Beneath him, around him
the water is a muscle,
a heart of jewels spilled over rock.
He's forgotten his hand on the paddle,
his arm dips and pulls, guides the boat
to enter the river, unnoticed.

He keeps his back turned
as his children pry effortlessly
through the rapids,
sure of their skill, that they feel
where the boat must go.
Still, there is a sadness
in his straight, impassive back,
as if by turning from them,
he insures they will go on
paddling forever, forever his,
here among lighted waters,
flexing, opening around him
in song.

*for Mickey Landry*

# About the Author

Jeanie Thompson has published two previous collections of poetry, *How to Enter the River* (1985, Holy Cow! Press) and *Witness* (1995, Black Belt Press, winner of the 1996 PMA Benjamin Franklin Award for Poetry/Literary Criticism). She has published three chapbooks, *Lotus and Psalm*, *Litany for a Vanishing Landscape*, and *Ascent*. Some poems from *White for Harvest* appeared in *Farewell to a Garden*, a limited edition chapbook printed in 1997.

Thompson's poems, reviews, and interviews with writers have appeared in *Alabama Literary Review, Amaryllis, Black Warrior Review, North American Review, Southern Humanities Review, Southern Review, Virginia Quarterly Review*, and other literary journals.

Since 1993 she has served as executive director of the Alabama Writers' Forum, a partnership program of the state's Council on the Arts. A native Alabamian, Thompson was the founding editor of the University of Alabama's literary periodical, *Black Warrior Review*. With Jay Lamar she coedited *The Remembered Gate: Memoirs by Alabama Writers*, a collection of auto-biographical essays to be published by the University of Alabama Press in 2002. She has received individual artist fellowships from the Louisiana Arts Council and the Alabama State Council on the Arts.